Confident Christianity

by Mark Meynell

Series Editor: Tim Chester

Confident Christianity
The good book guide to Colossians
© Mark Meynell/The Good Book Company, 2008.

The Good Book Company
Tel: 0845-225-0880
Fax: 0845-225-0990
Email: admin@thegoodbook.co.uk
Internet: www.thegoodbook.co.uk

ISBN: 978 1906334 24 6

Printed in China

CONTENTS

Introduction: Good Book Guides

Every Bible-study group is different—yours may take place in a church building, in a home or in a cafe, on a train, over a leisurely mid-morning coffee or squashed into a 30-minute lunch break. Your group may include new Christians, mature Christians, non-Christians, mums and tots, students, businessmen or teens. That's why we've designed these *Good Book Guides* to be flexible for use in many different situations.

Our aim in each session is to uncover the meaning of a passage, and see how it fits into the 'big picture' of the Bible. But that can never be the end. We also need to appropriately apply what we have discovered to our lives. Let's take a look at what is included:

⊕ **Talkabout:** most groups need to 'break the ice' at the beginning of a session, and here's the question that will do that. It's designed to get people talking around a subject that will be covered in the course of the Bible study.

⬇ **Investigate:** the Bible text for each session is broken up into manageable chunks, with questions that aim to help you understand what the passage is about. **The Leader's Guide** contains **guidance on questions**, and sometimes ☒ additional 'follow-up' questions.

⤓ **Explore more (optional):** these questions will help you connect what you have learned to other parts of the Bible, so you can begin to fit it all together like a jig-saw.

→ **Apply:** As you go through a Bible study, you'll keep coming across **apply** sections. The first part has questions to get the group discussing what the Bible teaching means in practice for you and your church. The second part, ⬚ **getting personal**, is an opportunity for you to think, plan and pray about the changes that you personally may need to make as a result of what you have learned.

⬆ **Pray:** We want to encourage prayer that is rooted in God's Word—in line with His concerns, purposes and promises. So each session ends with an opportunity to review the truths and challenges highlighted by the Bible study, and turn them into prayers of request and thanksgiving.

The **Leader's Guide** and introduction provide historical background information, explanations of the Bible texts for each session, ideas for **optional extra** activities, and guidance on how best to help people uncover the truths of God's Word.

Why study Colossians?

It happens all the time…

People who start out well as Christians can end up light-years from the gospel of Jesus Christ, caught up in weird and not-so-wonderful cults, movements and traditions. And not just individuals, but whole churches and church movements. They may still talk about Jesus, but their focus has shifted from the fundamental truths of who He is and what He has done to other things: rituals, rapturous experiences, morality, or an intense engagement with ideas and schools of thought. These other things become the focus of our Christianity. It seems that Jesus Christ and His saving death are no longer enough…

This kind of teaching was the reason Paul wrote his letter to the Colossian church. He recognised the fall-out of 'moving on' from the gospel – we become unsure of God's forgiveness because it no longer depends solely on Jesus; we become proud of what we do; and ultimately, these new ways of thinking and alternative spiritualities completely fail to deliver the new life and fulfillment that they promise.

But Paul shows us, not just the *better* way, but the *only true way* to grow and be fruitful as a Christian believer. And it starts by understanding exactly who Jesus Christ is – the God who created and sustains the world, indeed the very reason that we exist at all. The fact that this awesome ruler of the universe became a man and died to reconcile us to God is the heart of the Christian gospel that not only saves us, but is also the only basis for genuine Christian growth.

Undoubtedly, Christians today face the same danger. These six studies can help us resist the fine-sounding arguments enticing us to add to what Jesus has done. Only if we are convinced about the true identity of Christ, and certain that He alone is all we need to grow, will we mature into confident Christians.

The six studies in this Good Book Guide will help groups and individuals find the way to achieve true Christian growth into confidence and fruitfulness.

Colossians 1 v 1-14
JESUS OUR CONFIDENCE

⊕ talkabout

1. What things do you give thanks to God and/or pray for the most?

In his opening paragraphs, Paul tells the Colossians what is filling his prayers; and even though he has never met them, it is the Colossians themselves!

⊕ investigate

▶ Read Colossians 1 v 1-8

Having heard news of the Colossians from their friend Epaphras (v 7, 8), Paul is greatly encouraged because all the signs point to their walk with Jesus being genuine.

2. What evidence is there for the Colossians' conversion?

3. Read v 5. In what ways does hope motivate faith and love?

4. The New Testament describes conversion to Christ in various ways. What is unusual about Paul's description in v 5-8?

• Why is this change not simply a matter of intellectual understanding?

❯ Read 1 v 9-11

Paul's prayer moves naturally from thanking God to asking God, because he recognises that Epaphras' news is just the start. What matters now is how these Colossian Christians grow to maturity. We sometimes find it difficult to pray for people that we have never met. Paul has no such trouble, and his prayer takes us to the heart of what is most important in the Christian life.

5. What does Paul specifically pray for in v 9?

6. Why are these things important (see v 10-11)?

7. What is the link between knowledge, wisdom and good works (v 9-10)?

❯ Read 1 v 12-14

It's crucial to recognise that Paul is not expecting the Colossians to 'turn over a new leaf' in their lives as if they could suddenly decide to be good. The spiritual growth he prays for comes from a deeper appreciation of what God has already done for and in them.

8. Note the tense of these verses (past, present or future). List all the things that the Father has done. How did He achieve them?

9. So how can a Christian's have confidence when faced with the challenge to endure with patience and joy (see v 11)?

⊡ explore more

Read 1 Thessalonians 1 v 1-10.
• *What are the similarities and differences between Paul's prayers in this passage and the one in Colossians 1 v 3-14?*

⊟ apply

10. What are the challenges from this passage for our priorities in prayer?

11. What will the cost be for us, if we are to be faithful followers of Christ?

12. How can we contribute to the gospel bearing fruit?
(Clue: how did it bear fruit in the Colossians' life, v 8?)

⬆ pray

Thank God for:

- the gospel of grace, which gives spiritual failures confidence to live for God.

- those you know who live a life of faith, love and hope.

- the fact that the gospel is still bearing fruit all over the world (and thank Him for specific places you are familiar with).

Ask God:

- to deepen your knowledge of God's will so that you might live to please God.

- to bring others to hear and understand God's grace.

- to help you endure by His strengthening power.

Colossians 1 v 15-23
JESUS OUR LORD

⊕ talkabout

1. If they give Jesus any thought at all, how do your friends and colleagues tend to view Him? What relevance would they say that He has today?

Paul's description of Jesus Christ is packed with big surprises. Whatever our starting point, Jesus is far greater than we could ever have imagined. Allow yourself to be amazed and stretched by what you read here.

⊕ investigate

❯ Read 1 v 15-20

2. Underline or write down each time Paul uses the words 'all', 'every' and 'full'. What point is Paul making?

3. Spot the parallels between the two halves of this passage:

	v 15-17 – CREATION	v 18-20 – RESCUE
• How is Jesus described?		
• What does Jesus achieve?		

• Why is is it important for us that Jesus is God's image?

> Re-read v 13-17

4. Paul makes astonishing claims about what God has done through Jesus (v 13-14). What qualifies Jesus to bring about this rescue (v 15)?

5. How does the universe depend on Jesus? Describe the past and present aspects of this relationship.

6. Why does Paul spell out that Christ's authority even extends to human rulers (v 16. Clue: look at 4 v 18!)?

Having outlined Jesus' triumph in the creation of the universe, Paul now shifts to His triumph in rescuing the universe.

> Re-read v 18-20

7. Why is it important we understand that Jesus is the 'head of the body, the church'?

8. What is the extent of Jesus' victory on the cross?

• How does His death on the cross make peace?

⊡ **explore more**

Read John 1 v 1-14 and Hebrews 1 v 1-4. What do these passages add to our understanding of Jesus' identity and mission from Colossians 1.

⊟ **apply**

9. In the light of these verses, how might you respond to a Christian friend who says, 'Jesus simply died to forgive us'?

10. What would you say to a friend who considers Jesus irrelevant?

After the cosmic scope of the previous section, Paul now gets personal.

⊍ **investigate**

▶ **Read 1 v 21-23**

11. What has changed in the Colossians' lives and how did that come about?

12. What will a confident Christian look like from v 23?

⇨ apply

13. What difficulties do you face in proclaiming the gospel to others?

- How does this passage encourage and strengthen you for that?

⬆ pray

Thank God for:
- the confidence of knowing Jesus' cosmic authority as creator and rescuer.
- your own reconciliation to God.

Ask God:
- for the ability to continue in your faith, unmoved from the gospel's hope.
- to change the hearts of friends who fail to recognise Jesus' authority.

3

Colossians 1 v 24 – 2 v 7
JESUS OUR ROCK

⊕ talkabout

1. What things shake your confidence as a Christian?

Paul endured a great deal in his life – including insults, beatings and imprisonments – all for preaching Jesus.

⊕ investigate

▶ **Read 1 v 24-29**

2. What enabled Paul to persevere and even rejoice in the midst of his sufferings?

A 'mystery' in the bible is not something strange or spooky. Instead it is something that *was* secret but is now out in the open and public knowledge.

3. What exactly is the 'mystery' God has chosen to reveal to the Gentiles, and why is it so remarkable?

4. Spell out the part Paul plays in preaching the gospel and the part God plays. What is the ultimate goal in this partnership?

⊟ apply

5. What would you say to someone who feels intimidated by how people respond to their Christian faith? Would you listen to your own advice?

6. *'Christ in you, the hope of glory'*. Spell out the privileges of being a Christian. How can we help one another to be reminded of them?

⊡ explore more

> **Read Acts 16 v 16-34.**
How do we see Paul's teaching in Colossians being lived out in his life?

⊡ investigate

> **Read 2 v 1-7**

7. How can Paul be 'struggling for' the Colossians when he has never met them (see also Colossians 4 v 12)?

Confident Christianity

Paul's message is one that offers 'the full riches of complete understanding', and 'all the treasures of wisdom.' (2 v 2-3) Just as he did in chapter 1, Paul emphasises the truth that the gospel of Jesus provides everything we need for life with God.

8. Why is it so important for the Colossians to understand that the Gospel provides everything (2 v 4-5)?

9. What was Paul's advice to the Colossians in v 6-7? Try to summarise it in your own words:

⊟ apply

10. How can we be deceived into thinking that the message of Jesus is not enough for us?

11. Why is it important to be 'overflowing with thankfulness'?

⊡ getting personal

It is easy to say that Jesus is the centre of our lives – but how central is He to our daily decision-making, our ambitions and priorities in life?
* *Are you in all honesty seeking to follow Paul's commands in v 6-7?*
* *What could you do differently or start doing as a result?*

12. From what you have learned so far, discuss how to respond to the following 'fine-sounding arguments' so popular today.

- It is just intolerant, sinful pride to view your beliefs as current and true, and all others as false and wrong.

- Jesus isn't obsessed with religious categories. It doesn't matter to Him what faith a person chooses to label himself by. What matters is our love and service to our fellow men.

⬆ pray

Thank God:

- for the ways in which Jesus has been enough for you this week.

Ask God:

- to help you continue to live in Christ and to see through fine-sounding arguments.

4 Colossians 2 v 8-23
JESUS OUR FULLNESS

⊕ talkabout

1. What images spring to mind with words like 'holiness' and 'spirituality'?

Paul now draws together some of the big ideas from the last three sections – applying the significance of Jesus' identity more closely to the lives of the Colossians and the struggles they were facing.

⊕ investigate

❯ Read 2 v 8-15

2. In what ways is the message of Christ different from the hollow and deceptive philosophies of human tradition (v 8)?

Paul is not referring to pagan thinking here – in fact he is challenging the mindset that insists on Gentile converts to Christ having to keep the Jewish law (hence the imagery of circumcision).

3. What was the purpose of circumcision in the Old Testament (see Genesis 17 v 9-14)?

• So what does Paul mean by the 'circumcision done by Christ' (v 11)?

4. What three enemies are destroyed by Jesus death on the cross (v 13-15)? How has this been achieved?

5. How does the cross now make the desire to keep the Jewish law an expression of human tradition?

⊟ apply

6. Many today suggest that it is arrogant to be confident that you are right with God. How would you respond to them?

⊡ getting personal

The writer to the Hebrews speaks of having 'the full assurance of faith' (Hebrews 10 v 22). Is this something that you have?
• *If so, praise God for it! If not, what is preventing it?*

⊌ investigate

❯ Read 2 v 16-23

7. Why is the Jewish law no longer needed?

8. What are the spiritual dangers for someone who tries to keep the law in this way (v 17-19)?

9. Why does the rule-keeping referred to by Paul fail to have the desired effect? (v 20-23)

⊡ explore more

The relationship that Christians have to the Jewish law is a complex issue, since God had obviously been the one to reveal it! Jesus tackled precisely this issue in the Sermon on the Mount (Matthew 5 v 17-18)
• *How does Jesus understand His relationship to the law?*

➔ apply

10. Christians today can fall into the same trap as the false teachers in Colossae. What are some of the unnecessary rules or purely cultural conventions that we expect new Christians to keep?

- Is there anything you as an individual, or as a church, need to change or stop doing as a result?

11. Are you in danger of adding to Christ and His work? Look at the following statements. How do they make you feel, and how would you respond?

- 'If I don't start the day with prayer and reading my Bible, everything else goes wrong'

- 'Christians spend too much time talking to God, and not enough time just patiently waiting to hear His still, small voice.'

- 'I didn't feel I was truly following Christ until I gave up the trappings of materialism – my car, the TV, eating meat. The simple life brings me closer to God'

⊕ **pray**

Thank God

- For the freedom from human regulations and expectations that we have in Christ

Ask God

- To help you have the full assurance of faith, having confidence in Christ's finished work on the Cross.

5 Colossians 3 v 1 – 4 v 1
JESUS OUR LIFESTYLE

⊕ talkabout

1. If you were to ask someone what they think of churches and Christians they have known, how would they respond? Do you think their opinions are fair?

⊙ investigate

❯ Read 3 v 1-4

Paul has given us an astounding account of who Jesus is, and what He has done for us. He now spells out the implications of these truths for how His followers should think and therefore live.

2. What has already happened to believers?

• What will happen in the future to believers?

3. So what should be the thing that drives a Christian's thoughts and actions?

4. How is it possible to say that a Christian has already been raised with Christ? How can we know that this has happened?

> ▶ **Read 3 v 5-14**

5. Find the expressions that talk about giving up the old way of life. What does each of them mean?

6. Find the expressions that describe the way a believer should take up a new way of life. What extra motives to change does Paul mention here?

7. What do these phrases suggest that the change to living a new life will be like? What extra insight does v10 give to how this change takes place?

8. What should a church actually look like according to v 11-14? Why?

☺ getting personal

We all have our own areas of frequent temptation and failure. Which of the sins outlined in 3 v 5-11 are particular issues for you? Which virtues require particular effort? Make a concerted and prayerful effort to work on these in the coming week.

⤷ apply

9. What makes setting 'our hearts on things above' difficult? How can we encourage one another to keep a heavenly perspective?

10. How will these verses help you to resolve conflicts and disputes affecting the unity of your church or small group?

⤓ investigate

> ▶ **Read 3 v 15 – 4 v 1**

Paul now moves to more general recommendations for community life. Notice that these go beyond simply what we do in church together. This is about the whole of our lives, seven days a week.

11. What are the three essential ingredients for healthy life (v 15, 16, 17)?

12. Look through the 'household code' in 3 v 18 – 4 v 1. How does the Christian attitude to relationships differ from modern views about personal rights?

13. What Paul says here was just as challengingly counter-cultural in the first century as it is now. What is the most important truth for slaves and masters to remember? How does this affect their relationship?

Identify one personal relationship you are struggling with at the moment. What command do you need to obey?

If you are able, share the need with the group to pray for and encourage you.

⬆ **pray**

Thank God:

- for the joy of knowing that if you know Christ, you have been raised with Him and that you are a member of God's chosen people, holy and dearly loved.

- for the change that God has already begun to bring in your life.

Ask God

- for the ability to set your heart on things above and thus to put off the old self and put on the new self.

- for God's peace to rule and God's word to dwell richly in your heart.

- for the life of the Christian community that you belong to.

6 Colossians 4 v 2-18
JESUS OUR MINISTRY

⊕ talkabout

1. Who are the people who have influenced you most in your Christian walk? What aspects of their lives and ministry made them such an influence?

⊕ investigate

> **Read 4 v 2-6**

Having spent some time teaching about building authentic Christian communities, Paul now turns his attention to our relationship with God and the world beyond the church.

2. How do these verses give us guidance in our prayer priorities and our outreach?

3. What is the significance of Paul's use of the expression 'the mystery of Christ' (compare with 1 v 27)?

4. Despite the costs involved, why can we be confident when we share the gospel with others?

⊟ apply

5. What practical steps can we take to ensure:

• we pray with these priorities?

• we are proclaiming the mystery of Christ clearly?

• we fill our conversation with the salt of grace?

⊥ investigate

▶ **Read 4 v 7-18**

While we might find a passage like this harder to relate to than some others, we should remember that it would have brought real encouragement to the Colossians. Even here, though, there are many things to learn.

6. What virtues do the individuals Paul mentions have in common?

7. What do we learn about the nature of, and priorities for prayer from the description of Epaphras in v 12-13?

8. Why do you think Paul signs off with a reminder of his chains (v 18)?

⊡ **explore more**

❯ **Read v 14, and 2 Timothy 4 v 10.**

• *What can we learn from the story of Demas?*

⊡ **getting personal**

Is there a person or a group that you are wrestling in prayer for? If not, start now! Determine to pray regularly, passionately and persistently for them.

⊡ **apply**

9. Paul's description of his friends focuses on their hard work and service for the gospel. How can we encourage one another to persevere in our service of the Lord, His people and those who do not yet know Him?

10. How does the prayer of Epaphras (v 12) sum up the big message of the letter to the Colossians? Write a sentence summarising the main point Paul has been trying to convey to them.

11. What advice would you give the following people from Colossians?
- A timid young Christian who wants to be more confident as a believer.

- Someone who claims to have discovered 'something new' in the Christian life.

- Someone who wants to know how to grow as a Christian.

⊼ **pray**

Thank God:
- for the open doors God has provided us for passing the gospel on to others.
- for the individuals who have made an impact on your own Christian walk.

Ask God:
- for watchful and thankful prayer lives.
- for opportunities to explain the mystery of Christ.
- to give you the desire and strength to work hard and sacrificially in the work of Christ.

Confident Christianity

LEADER'S GUIDE

Colossians 1 v 1-14
JESUS OUR CONFIDENCE

THE BIG IDEA
Growing in the Christian life is about understanding and relying on what God has done for us in Christ.

SUMMARY
Colossae was in what is now southwest Turkey, not far from Laodicea and near the great Ephesus road. Paul writes this letter from his prison in Rome to a church that he has never visited, but about which he has heard fantastic reports from their leader and founder, Epaphras (compare 1 v 7, 4 v 12). He writes the letter both to encourage and to alert the church to the dangers of false teachers (some of whom have sought to infiltrate the church). They had started well in their Christian walk – they clearly understood the relationship between Christian faith, love and hope (1 v 4-5) and this provided them a firm foundation for their lives in Christ. The important thing is that they continue to understand and trust in Christ's victory at the cross (1 v 12-13), which will then impact their daily living (1 v 9-11). This is why Paul is so keen to pray for them and to write this letter.

GUIDANCE ON QUESTIONS
1. If you keep a prayer diary as a group, it may be worth reading out some of the things you have regularly prayed for. The point of this exercise is to show that the things we often pray for – illness, guidance questions etc – are very different from the things Paul prays for.

2. Epaphras has reported the significant difference that the Colossians' conversions have made to their lives. They responded to the gospel with trust in Christ and a love for fellow believers (note: 'saints' in the Bible are all those in Christ and not those who have reached a higher grade of discipleship).

3. Christian hope marks the gospel out as unique – for it brings total confidence in an eternal future, simply because of what Christ has achieved on our behalf. We contribute nothing. If we did, there could be no confidence. As we consider this future, we are thrown back on Christ's mercy and recognise we have no option but to trust Him. This then gives us the freedom to love others without the burden of trying to earn God's approval.

4. Strangely, Paul talks about the gospel (like a living thing – a seed growing and bearing fruit) as the most important thing.
• Conversion here is described as hearing 'the word of truth' (v 5), understanding 'God's grace in all its truth' (v 6) and learning 'it from Epaphras' (v 7). There is therefore an intellectual element to conversion. But it can never stop there – for it leads to 'love in the Spirit' (v 8), which is evidence of a changed life.

5. He prays that God would fill them with 'the knowledge of His will', and give them 'all spiritual wisdom and understanding'. Knowing God's will comes through the wisdom and knowledge of God that we derive from the gospel.

6. Because the false teachers in Colossae were undermining the completed work of Christ (as we will soon see), it was essential for Paul to root these believers in the gospel. Firm convictions were needed if they were to bear fruit and grow (v 10), and especially to endure (v 11). Note that this is not philosophical knowledge – it is about a relationship with God.

7. Throughout the Bible, there is a clear link between doctrine and ethics, between what we think and how we behave. Wrong thinking invariably leads to wrong living. This is all the more true when it comes to our understanding of the character of God.

8. The past tenses are the key to a Christian's assurance. They point us to the reality that God has already done everything we need to be saved: He 'qualified' us for heaven (v 12), 'rescued' us from darkness (v 13), and 'brought' us into the kingdom of the Son (v 13). These were all ultimately achieved at the cross – where Jesus, once and for all time, completed His divine rescue mission.

9. We all have days when the going gets tough. But because God is the one who has achieved the victory (v 13), a Christian's ability to endure, whatever gruelling challenges lie ahead, is all about depending on what God has done for us in Christ.

EXPLORE MORE:

In **1 Thessalonians 1 v 1-10**, Paul also focuses his thanksgiving to God on the outworking of these Christians' faith, love and hope (1 Thessalonians 1 v 3). Just as with the Colossians, each of these three virtues has practical impact, producing 'work',

'labour' and 'endurance'. Furthermore, there is a parallel in the difference that their hope makes – for that is what enables them to serve the living and true God (as opposed to dumb idols) as they wait for Jesus' return (1 Thessalonians 1 v 9-10).

But there are subtle differences between the two passages. In Colossians, he is already flagging up some of his concerns about their gospel convictions. Verses 11-14 suggest that the Colossians were looking elsewhere for strength to endure. In 1 Thessalonians, Paul is thrilled about the impact their conversions have had on the wider church (eg: 1 Thessalonians 1 v 8). Both churches have started well, and this has given Paul real encouragement and grounds for praise.

🔟 **What grounds for encouragement and praise do you find in your church?**

10. APPLY: Prayer priorities: Compare your answers to Q1! Will we share Paul's commitment to praying for Christians' wisdom and gospel understanding?

11. Discipleship costs: we need endurance not only in tough circumstances (which Paul clearly assumes will come), but also our challenge is, daily, to find strength and joy in God rather than always trying to avoid suffering and difficulty.

12. The gospel bore fruit in the Colossians life when they heard and understood the Grace of God, and showed love in the Spirit. We can support gospel growth by:
• teaching the gospel ourselves.
• supporting preachers like Epaphras.
• praying for gospel growth and fruit in the lives of others
• demonstrating the fruit of the gospel in our lives (ie: love, holiness, joy etc.).

Colossians 1 v 15-23

JESUS OUR LORD

THE BIG IDEA

We can be confident in Jesus because of who He is: the full and final word for knowing God's character, authority and purposes in his world; and for what He has done: reconciled a rebellious world to God through his death on the cross.

SUMMARY

The false teachers in Colossae clearly undermined core gospel truths. It is not that they never talked about Jesus. The problem was that they subtly shifted people's focus from the biblical and historical Jesus. They undermined his full identity and finished work on the cross, by implying that coming to Christ in conversion was not enough to have confidence for the future and eternity. So in these momentous paragraphs, Paul lifts our eyes to the wonders of who Jesus is and what he has done. Having done that, he unpacks the astounding confidence that is every Christian's right and privilege. This provides the foundation for the next section: stick to Jesus for the whole of your Christian walk; don't think you can graduate from him (see Col 2v6-7)

Note: 'Reconcile all things' (v 20). Some people may raise the question of whether all people are saved because of the wording in this verse. It is true that one day the whole of creation will be united in recognising the Lordship of Jesus (See Philippians 2 v 11). But as the following verses in Colossians make plain, there are still two ways to go.

Those who love him will bow the knee gladly, those who have rejected Him must still be judged.

OPTIONAL EXTRA

Consider a cinematic or TV portrayal of Christ that you have all seen, perhaps showing a clip from one of them. How does it help or hinder our understanding of Jesus' identity and mission? What value (if any) is there in such attempts to portray Christ?

GUIDANCE ON QUESTIONS

2. Paul is stressing the sufficiency of Jesus for everything – He is fully God; He made everything and is the redeemer of everything; He thus has authority over everything; He sustains everything; He is the first to rise from the dead; He brings real and lasting peace with God.

3. See table opposite for answers.
• Being 'God's image' effectively means that he makes the invisible God visible. He provides the greatest window into the character and purposes of God that the world has ever known. See John 14 v

Note: being 'firstborn over all creation' in no sense implies that he is a part of creation, as if he was the same as all other creatures. Not only would that contradict everything Paul says in this paragraph; but it also misunderstands the term. To be firstborn in the ancient world meant being the primary inheritor in the family. Jesus

	1 v 15-17 – Creation	1 v 18-20 – Rescue
How is Jesus described?	• Image of the invisible God • Firstborn over all creation • He is before all things	• Head of the body, the church • Firstborn from among the dead • God pleased to have all His fullness dwell in Him
What does Jesus achieve?	• All things created by Him (and that really does mean everything!) • All things created for Him • All things hold together in Him	• Firstborn from among the dead (so has supremacy) • God pleased… to reconcile all things to Himself • Made peace through His blood, shed on the cross

thus has a Son's rights (compare 1 v 12-13) over all creation because of who He is, but also because He is its creator.

4. Most people have no difficulty with the concept of God creating and sustaining the universe. What is truly mind-blowing is the Bible's claim that this same creating, all-sustaining God became a human being, none other than Jesus of Nazareth.

5. Past: Jesus was the one at the beginning: He was before all things, He created all things. **Present:** He holds everything together, and it is for Him that everything exists.

6. Paul was writing from prison (see 4 v 18). The Roman world was hostile to the gospel and its messengers. In the face of such persecution, it was vital to cling to a confidence in the sovereignty of Christ. His lordship extends even to those who sent Paul to prison in the first place. While there are things that are hard to understand about this truth, we can draw real comfort in the midst of suffering.

7. If we don't acknowledge that Jesus is the head of the church, then we will inevitably go wrong. We will make reason, or tradition or our leaders into the head, and so compromise the purpose and character of the church. It seems from chapter 2 that this is the danger the Colossians were wrestling with. If Jesus is Lord of the church, then His word will be our rule and guide.

8. The surprise is that Jesus' victory is cosmic: 'all things' (whether on earth or in heaven) are reconciled.
• Human rebellion against God caused a profound dislocation and rupture throughout God's creation. Jesus' death repairs and restores it all. Peace comes because of the shedding of His blood – biblical shorthand for His death in our place, taking the punishment for rebellion we deserve onto Himself, so that we might be restored to friendship with God. If people are unfamiliar with these truths, Hebrews 9 v 19-26 expresses them clearly.

EXPLORE MORE
These three passages are the classic New

Testament witnesses to Jesus' Incarnation – where he is clearly seen to be both fully divine and fully human. **John 1** echoes Genesis 1 and has a similar cosmic scope to Colossians 1. We see that:

- the Creator God of Genesis is none other than the Word himself – who is God
- God became human when he made his dwelling among us. John 1 v 14 literally means he 'tabernacled' with us, picking up on Old Testament imagery of the place where people went to meet with God: the tabernacle/temple.

Hebrews 1 has a focus on how Jesus completes the process of revelation, which started in the Old Testament:

9. APPLY: The key is the cosmic scope of God's purposes – the cross is not simply about forgiving someone or 'getting them to heaven'. It is designed, in one great decisive victory, to restore everything in the universe to the Lordship of Christ.

10. Jesus is not just a 'special friend' for Christians. The resurrection here points to Jesus' supremacy. He is the Lord of all, whether people recognise that or not, whether you think He is relevant or not. What Jesus achieved is the only way that all the problems and agonies of the fallen world will be overcome.

11. The alienation from God experienced by the whole of creation had been the experience of the individual Colossians as well. But through hearing the gospel of the victorious death of Christ, they were reconciled to God and presented 'holy in his sight'. This is what they are to continue trusting in.

12. A confident Christian will:
- **'continues' in their faith**. That is, they

continue to believe the truths of the Gospel and also live by it. The truth that Jesus Christ is the Lord of all and the very purpose for the existence of the world will be the truth that dominates their decisions and choices.
- **'be steadfast'.** That is, they will be prepared to fight or contend for this truth, even when it costs them. They will hold to it even if they are persecuted for it. They won't just follow the latest fad in spirituality or go looking for other things outside Jesus, because everything is in Him
- **'not moved from the hope of the Gospel.'** That is, they are confident that in Christ they are fully accepted by God and sure that they will live with Him forever. This gives them the ability to endure suffering and hardship now, and happy not to seek after everything the world has to offer, because they know that they will have it all and more besides, in eternity with Christ.

13. APPLY: Many people are either ignorant of, or couldn't care less about, the claims of Christ. What's more, many have precious little hope for the future. This passage reminds us of God's cosmic purposes – and the fact that in Christ he has already won. People's rejection of him doesn't change that fact. We are simply servants of the message of Jesus' Lordship (as Paul was in 1v23). To put it bluntly, Christ's Lordship does not depend on my ability or failures in passing on the message.

Prayer
Make sure that you spend time in praise and worship to the Lord Jesus for all He is and has done for us.

3 Colossians 1 v 24 – 2 v 7
JESUS OUR ROCK

THE BIG IDEA
Because Jesus is fully God and His victory is total, it is fruitless and foolish to move on from Him – instead we should grow deeper roots in Him.

SUMMARY
Paul was prepared to suffer in order to proclaim Christ because it meant building up His body (the church). For Paul, the real privilege was to explain the wonders of God's purposes to the non-Jewish or Gentile world: namely that a Jewish Messiah (or king) was in fact the ruler of the universe. Jesus is the focal point for all Christian ministry. Even though such ministry brings hardships, Paul is confident that God is at work in Him, providing all the energy he needs to carry out his ministry.

The threat to the Colossians' faith is what particularly provokes Paul to write this letter. There are those who undermine Jesus' finished work by saying that a believer needs to supplement what Christ has done, perhaps through wisdom that is to be found elsewhere (compare 2 v 3-4). But such people deceive by their 'fine-sounding arguments'. Paul would love to teach the Colossians in person – but for the time being he can only write. The heart of his message is therefore in 2 v 6-7 – don't move on from Christ; go deeper into Christ.

OPTIONAL EXTRA
Find a hymn or song that faces up to the realities of suffering and disappointment in the Christian life. Play it to, or sing it with, the group and discuss the extent to which it puts suffering in a right, biblical perspective. (Eg: Hymns: *Abide with me*; *Father hear the prayer we offer*. Modern songs are harder to find on these themes, but try: Matt Redman's *Blessed Be Your Name* or Stuart Townend's *We Have Sung Our Songs Of Victory*.)

GUIDANCE ON QUESTIONS
1. Try to draw out a whole range of issues.
• Intellectual attacks, eg: documentaries or books that cast doubt on the Bible or the historicity of Jesus.
• Disappointments, eg: the failures of Christian leaders that you look up to.
• Seemingly inexplicable suffering.
Pastoral note: Listen carefully to what people say, as it may reveal real issues they are struggling with. People can often talk in an abstract way about something that they are really wrestling with deep inside. Make a note to follow up on anything that has raised concern with a personal conversation.

2. In no sense did Paul enjoy suffering nor did he rejoice at the fact of other people suffering. That would be absurd. Suffering is simply part of Christian discipleship, but the joy is to be found in the perspective and the purpose that Christ gives suffering. Paul suffered for his efforts to make the gospel known to the Gentile world. Knowing that they now know 'this mystery' (v 27) is what makes it all worthwhile and joyful.

3. The 'mystery' is about Christ being made known to the whole world, including the Gentiles. Remarkably, the God who made the universe and sustains it chooses to make His home in us and to take us to glory.

4. • God's Part: The church is Christ's body – it is His agent on earth. He is the one suffering through its sufferings (compare with Paul's conversion experience in Acts 9 v 4) but He is therefore also the one to commission the preaching of the gospel. It is His mystery that was hidden and now disclosed by God (v 27). He is the one who works powerfully within His agents as they proclaim (v 29).
• **Paul's part:** In the light of that, Paul and all who follow him in Christian ministry are merely servants, who seek to present the word faithfully and in its fulness (v 25), and must be prepared to suffer for it (v 24).
• **The goal** is for men and women to be presented perfect in Christ (1 v 28) – it is disciples that God seeks, not merely converts.

5. APPLY: This is a totally understandable fear – it would be strange if we didn't feel it. However, we are called to follow Jesus – we can't expect to avoid something of what He endured (cf John 15 v 20). That never means He has abandoned us or that what we go through is indefinite or futile. Colossians constantly reminds us of God's sovereign plan and sustaining power for those who trust in Him.

6. APPLY: In the present, we have the astonishing confidence of 'Christ in you'.

That idea dovetails with the idea of a Christian being 'in Christ' (1 v 28). There is a strong sense of security in knowing both truths. Then we have the future perspective given by 'the hope of glory' – this is no pipe-dream but confidence because it all depends on God. Still, this can all seem unreal when things get tough. That is why we need to read our Bibles, be part of Christian meetings and be involved in Christian service – so that we are constantly drawn back to spiritual realities.

EXPLORE MORE
In this passage in Acts, we see Paul and Silas preaching the gospel in Philippi. Their experience is one of acceptance, opposition and hostility as the gospel does its work. The first three converts are a wealthy businesswoman, a possessed slave girl and a rough jailer and his family - a remarkable group, showing how the gospel of God reaches out to everyone. Paul and Silas bear their suffering with joy – singing hymns in the stocks – and God wonderfully blesses their faithful witness.

7. Long distances are no bar to Paul's ministry to the Colossian Christians, nor is the fact that he has never met them. Presumably (from the reference to Epaphras in 4 v 12), Paul is struggling on their behalf by devoted prayer for them, as well as by writing this letter to them. But see also 2 v 4! Paul is struggling for them by contending for the true gospel message. This encourages Christians everywhere (1 v 23).

8. If we don't understand the fullness of what we have in Christ, we will be easy prey for the deceptions of false teachers because they are offering to supplement Christ with their own ways of thinking or living, which will offer an easier life, or giver room for our own pride. The rule is that if you try to add to Jesus, you will always end up taking away from His achievements, because, if you have to add anything, it suggests that what He did was inadequate in the first place.

9. Stick with Jesus! There is always more to learn and love about Christ. Continue to grow by being grounded where you started – hence the imagery of a tree putting down strong roots. Thankfulness is a key discipline here because, when we start to look for things to be thankful for, we will always find more than enough in Jesus!

10. APPLY: How are we deceived? It usually starts with making us dissatisfied with the realities of the Christian life, eg: our struggle with sin. They then offer us a 'better way' that will help us over the problem. That's why thankfulness is so important. If we are thankful to God for all He has given us, including the opportunity to suffer for Him, then we will not be dissatisfied, and hence prone to deception by false teachers.

There are many examples of this kind of false teaching around. Some say it doesn't matter which religion you turn to for hope – this denies the uniqueness of Christ and implies that we can be reconciled to God without the cross. But some within Christian circles insist that a spiritual experience they have enjoyed should be the norm for all Christians. This can leave people feeling insecure and that somehow their walk with Jesus is lacking. But if we are in Christ, we have it all already, regardless of how we feel or what we experience.

11. APPLY: Gratitude is not just a good thing; it is a key Christian discipline. When we start to look for things to be thankful to God for, we will always find more than enough in Jesus! So it is something that we should do, even if we are not 'feeling thankful'. It strengthens us against those who would deceive us into thinking we need more than Jesus.

12. APPLY: Each of these arguments attacks the uniqueness of the gospel in reconciling sinners to God. Each one is a deceptive means of giving other faiths and creeds equality with the gospel. The arguments can appear 'fine-sounding' because they use half-truths.
• We can be intolerant and sinfully proud about our beliefs, BUT the key issue is truth. How can we know the gospel is true?
• Jesus isn't obsessed with religious categories (because all religion fails to reconcile us to God). BUT He calls people of all beliefs to put faith in Him alone.

It is important to underline to your group that false teaching will always be plausible in this way, because it will contain things that are true. We need to sort out the truth from the error.

Colossians 2 v 8-23
JESUS OUR FULLNESS

THE BIG IDEA
Christ has done everything we need to be reconciled to God through His death on the cross. If we add anything to Christ, we will only subtract our confidence!

SUMMARY
Paul now goes into much greater detail about the nature of the false teaching prevalent in Colosse. Because of his need to explain the issue of circumcision (2 v 11), it seems clear that a central element of this was the expectation for Gentile converts to keep the Jewish law in its entirety. The arguments for doing this would have seemed sensible and convincing (compare 2 v 4), not least because of course, the Old Testament law was God's idea in the first place. But Paul uses shocking language to describe the false teachers' approach: for despite the law's divine origins, their insistence on applying it directly to new Gentile believers renders their philosophy one of 'human tradition and the basic principles of this world (2 v 8).

The key reason for Paul's robust language is that to insist on people adopting human traditions as well as the gospel completely undermines Jesus' victorious achievements at the cross, which in turn undermines a Christian's sense of assurance. The cross is no longer 'enough' to be reconciled to God if a believer has to do certain things in addition. What is more, it tends to feed personal pride and loosens a person's wholehearted dependence on Christ.

Finally, and most depressingly, this approach completely fails to deliver what it promises, namely a lifestyle that is more Christ-like, holy or devoted.

It is vital that the Colossian believers resist this way of thinking. They should not feel pressured or insecure because they do not keep certain festivals or rituals (2 v 16-17). What matters is what they have in Christ.

OPTIONAL EXTRA
Think of any soap opera or movie characters who are supposed to be Christians. What impression do they give? How accurate is it? How much would you say this is a result of the writers' prejudice, and how much is actually deserved?

GUIDANCE ON QUESTIONS
1. Common ideas of holiness and spirituality include: people who are disconnected from the world, abstinence, emptying your mind, visions, ecstatic singing, killjoys, etc.

2. The key thing to identify is the *origin* of the way of life offered. Christ is from God; the alternatives are all of human invention. Whatever the roots of a particular way of life, if it undermines the work of Christ, then it is by definition not from God. For in Christ, we have God in all His fullness, and if we are Christian, we have Christ in all His fullness. The other major difference would be that the alternatives will sound great, whereas the true gospel will not pull any punches about how difficult it will be.

3. Circumcision was a physical sign of the covenant between God and His people. It showed that you belonged to God's chosen people. It marked you out as different.

• Instead of a physical act to demonstrate belonging to the community of God, Jesus now does this spiritually – at our conversion when we first trusted Him ('through your faith in the power of God' (2 v 12). You could see this as simply an alternative description of someone who has Christ in them (1 v 27) and is in Christ (1 v 28).

4. Through His death, He brought forgiveness and reconciliation to God by removing the three major obstacles that lie in a sinner's way:
• **death,** which is the inevitable consequence of rebellion against God (2 v 13).
• **our failure to obey God's standards** of perfection as expressed in the law (the 'written code … that stood opposed to us' – 2 v 14).
• **the powers and authorities** that stand opposed to God and His people (2 v 15).

He did this by:
• rising from the dead and enabling those in Christ to follow suit (2 v 13).
• taking the punishment deserved by spiritual failures on himself at the cross (2 v 14) – sin is never punished twice which is why we no longer have anything to fear.
Far from being a defeat, ironically, the cross was where God overcame hostile spiritual forces. Paul uses the imagery of a Roman triumph – a great procession of captured enemies through the streets of Rome.

5. We are naturally drawn to any religion that expects us to contribute good works

to earn a place with God, since it appeals to our innate pride in thinking that our contribution will have an impact. But according to Paul, that is deceptive, hollow, and worldly. Our sin is so serious that it leaves us spiritually dead (2 v 13) – we cannot possibly contribute anything. We are in dire need of a rescuer – which thankfully we find in Jesus (2 v 14-15). Going back to these religious ways of feeling safe, or helping us feel good about ourselves is not only not helpful, but positively harmful.

6. APPLY: The irony is that it is only those who rely on their own performance who are arrogant. To accept that we are in desperate need of forgiveness and that Christ is the only one to pull us out of our predicament requires great humility. However, confidence is a different matter altogether. For the truth is, confidence is only possible if we trust God to do everything we need to be reconciled. If it depended on us for even the smallest part, that confidence would instantly evaporate. Christian assurance is based on what Christ has already done on our behalf, not on what we can do for Him.

7. The law was a 'shadow' of the things that were to come in Jesus. Once He is here, we have the 'reality'. There is no need to return to them (2 v 16). Eg: The sacrificial system no longer applies because Jesus is the final sacrifice; the food laws no longer apply because we now show that we are different to the rest of the world by living a life of love for God and others.

8. Their humility will be a sham, because they are still arrogantly relying on their own performance to some degree. The 'worship of angels' seems to correspond to a strand of false teaching that made much of spiritual experiences: the danger with these is that they only lead further down the path to spiritual pride (2 v 18) as well as making others feel left out. Worst of all, a focus on personal achievement and experiences erodes dependence on Christ – which eventually leads to losing connection with Him altogether (2 v 19).

ⓘ **Share examples of this that you may have seen happen with other Christians, churches, or even in your own church.**

9. Such rules might help false teachers determine who is in their clique and who is out. But these distinctions have no value from an eternal perspective because they are 'based on human commands' (2 v 20-22). The make someone appear to be holy but they do nothing to deal with the sinful nature that is at work beneath the surface. The crucial point here is that sin can show itself in very religious ways, just as it can in pagan or irreligious ways.

EXPLORE MORE:
Jesus was frequently accused of undermining or abolishing the Old Testament law. He clearly refutes that by saying that He has come to fulfil the law, not least because it was God-given. However, His fulfilment of the law has many aspects:

- He fulfils the purpose for which it was given – for example, the sacrificial system was designed to be a shadow of what Jesus would achieve on the cross. So even though it is no longer in use, we need to study it in order to understand the cross.
- Uniquely, He keeps the law perfectly – He alone succeeded where the Old Testament people of God failed.
- He took on Himself the requirements of the law by suffering the punishment demanded by human failure to be holy.

10. APPLY: Our tendency is to twist the good gifts of God and wise habits of the Christian life into things that cause us spiritual problems. So for instance, we can easily twist the habit of having a regular devotional time with God into something that determines our status before God. We can think that if we have a quiet time, our day will automatically go better than if we don't, or that God will be more impressed with us. But our standing before God depends entirely on Christ's performance not ours! We do this with going to church, telling people about Jesus, seeking to be godly, acts of service and mercy and so on.

Pastoral note: Beware of any tendency in your group to point the finger at others without spending time thinking about how you as individuals, and as a church, may be making the same errors. The opposite danger here is that people use this opportunity for grumbling about things they feel are wrong with your own church. There may be legitimate concerns, but always make sure that any issues are properly dealt with by discussing with your church leadership, rather than just grumbling about them and leaving it. That can only be counter productive.

11. The three statements reflect the three different ways of adding to Christ's work highlighted in these verses:
- **Legalism (v 16-7):** law keeping makes me feel more acceptable to God.
- **Mysticism (v 18-19):** spiritual experiences make me feel more acceptable to God
- **Asceticism (v 20-23):** self-denial make me feel more acceptable to God.

People who talk like this can make us feel guilty or unconfident. Help the group see that these are steps backward, not forward!

5

Colossians 3 v 1 – 4 v 1
JESUS OUR LIFESTYLE

THE BIG IDEA
A Christian's lifestyle will reflect the victory that Christ has already won on our behalf. There is no aspect of our personal, family and community life and relationships that will not be changed.

SUMMARY
Being rescued by Jesus and having complete assurance as the result of His finished reconciling work is no excuse for an unchanged life. He is now our Lord. He did it all in order to restore everything in the universe to its rightful place under His authority (cf 1 v 18). We have been raised with Christ and therefore need to live lives that reflect that (3 v 1-4 then 3 v 5). This impacts our ambitions and desires, our words and deeds. It especially affects our relationships with fellow-believers, amongst whom there should be no discrimination (3v11) or division (3v12-14). If that is to happen, then we will need to depend on Christ all the more and work hard at serving Him and His people through everything. (3v15-18).

But this lifestyle revolution will not only affect our Christian communities. It must impact our homes as well – hence Paul's encouragements to the members of the typical household of his day: wives and husbands, parents and children, slaves and masters. These are all to be characterised by selfless service and other-person-centredness, just as the life of Jesus was.

OPTIONAL EXTRA
Give pairs of people the following scenarios, and get them to stage a one-minute drama for the rest of the group. The aim is to introduce the idea of conflict and the way people argue for their personal rights.
• **A boss and an employee:** one arguing for a pay rise, the other bringing out poor effort and time-keeping at work
• **A child and a parent:** a 'discussion' about staying out later than usual.
• **A husband and wife:** talking about the household budget overspend.
You may like to discuss these scenarios at the end to see what difference it would make if the parties were following Paul's teaching.

GUIDANCE ON QUESTIONS
1. Answers may include: full of hypocrites, people who need a psychological crutch; so heavenly-minded they are no earthly use (but see verse 2!); outdated; weird.
▣ **Why do people have such a bad impression of church?**

2. We died with Christ (v 3) and we were raised with Christ (v 1). Our real life is safe with Christ in heaven (v 3). All this is in the past tense. It is done and finished!
• In the future, when Jesus appears – a reference to His second coming – we will be taken to be with Him.

3. In chapter 2, Paul outlines the finished work of Jesus and the confidence a Christian can have as a result. In chapter 3, he spells out the implications this must have for everyday living. Because we have been raised with Christ (3 v 1), we should raise our sights to where He is and where one day we will be. As a result, we will inevitably want to live in a way that reflects where we belong (heaven, not this world) and to whom we belong (Jesus Christ is our master – no-one else!).

4. Paul deliberately blows our minds with this language! It is in the past tense because of what has already been achieved at the cross and resurrection. It is now as if there is a seat reserved in heaven for each person in Christ and marked with each person's name (3 v 3-4). Of course we cannot see this yet – but we trust in God's promises supremely because of His track-record in Christ.

5. 'Put to death' (v 5) suggests that we must try to kill off our old way of thinking that leads to ungodly living.
• **'Used to walk'** (v 7) makes us think of our life as a way to be and make choices each day – our daily walk.
• **'Rid yourselves'** (v 8) like throwing out the old rubbish .
• **'Taken off'** (v 9) like removing and discarding an old set of filthy clothes.

6. 'Put on the new self' (v 10) like clothing ourselves in new robes, fitting our new status as God's children (Galatians 3 v 27).
Our motivations should be driven by:

• The coming just judgment of God (v 6). He has made it known what displeases Him so it is surely now our concern to live in such a way that avoids that.
• The fact that He has chosen us, demonstrated His love for us in undeserved and unimaginable ways,

and that consequently we are forgiven completely (v 12-14).

7. Hard work! Growing in godliness will mean that we must struggle, fight and wrestle with our old natures. But the fight always starts with getting our head in the right place first! Understanding who we now are, the greatness of Jesus whom we are serving, and our ultimate destiny – the new creation. Verse 10 suggests that the renewal that is taking place is God's work in us. In other words, as we work, God is also working to effect this change.

8. As members of God's people, we must treat one another as Christ has treated us. This means that a church that is seeking to follow its Lord will be filled with people growing in Christ-likeness. Filled with truth and love. And absolutely no partiality on racial or social lines – because in His choosing of people, God shows no such distinction. Such a community is truly evangelistic!

9. APPLY: The heavenly world seems unreal because it is invisible. But a Christian needs constant reminders to see beyond the material and visible – reality is much bigger than what we see or feel! We need the Bible's reminders but we also need the challenges of fellow-believers who live lives that demonstrate a different set of values to those around us. Seeing someone resisting worldly ambitions or influences for the sake of Christ can make a profound impact – this is one reason for reading biographies of people who have done just that.

10. APPLY: Solving problems of disunity must start with ourselves – are there people we need to forgive or treat gently and kindly? We must avoid being quick to assume that divisions are other people's fault! Thinking like that could actually be part of the problem!

Pastoral note: Make sure that your group seeks to change their own lives, rather than push the blame elsewhere.

11. The three elements are:

- **The peace of Christ (v 15):** Our reconciliation to God through Christ (1 v 20) must lead to reconciliation with one another (cf 3 v 13).
- **The word of Christ (v 16):** Without this, it would be practically impossible to set our hearts on things above (3 v 1), such is the lure of the world. Notice how this word should permeate not just our teaching but also our singing.
- **Gratitude to God (v 15, v 17):** This is no afterthought but is essential if we are to remember our dependence on God and what He has done for us. Once we are reminded of that, any sense of superiority over others is completely erased.

12. Each person is to be characterised by an other-person-centredness. This will obviously look different on account of the fact that we all have different roles within a home – that of the child is not the same as that of the parent! There are controversies here of course, but if we take the section as a whole, we can see how it subverts modern assumptions about personal rights. In that sense, the whole passage is counter-cultural today.

Pastoral note: Now will not be the time to go into submission and roles in marriage. Paul deals with this more extensively in Ephesians 5-6. If it will help to defuse a potential argument, simply note that in Paul's introduction to this question of headship and order in marriage, his first command in Ephesians 5 v 21 is that everyone should submit to everyone else out of reverence for Christ.

13. The most vital relationship for both slave and master is the one each has with Jesus as Lord. That gives both individuals a heavenly perspective on how they relate to one another. Paul's instructions for the slave illustrate a vital truth about worship, namely, that the whole of life is about our dedication and service of God (v 23). It doesn't matter how menial or irrelevant it might seem to us. What is more, God's justice is perfect, which is something that both slaves and masters (and in contemporary terms, employees and employers) need constantly to remember (3 v 25 – 4 v 1).

PRAYER

The *Getting Personal* section in the study guide suggests that group members share a need in one of the relationship areas outlined in this passage. Make sure to keep these needs confidential, and to do what you can to follow up and support people with areas they are struggling with.

Try to bring your prayers always back the gospel motivation we should have to live a new life in Christ.

Colossians 4 v 2-18
JESUS OUR MINISTRY

THE BIG IDEA
When the gospel bears fruit in our lives we will be dependent on God through prayer, actively seeking opportunities to proclaim the gospel to the world around, and working together and standing firm as a body of believers.

SUMMARY
These final paragraphs are no afterthought. While they might at first seem to be a random collection of greetings and advice, there is a common thread. They all illustrate real life for those who trust the full revelation of God in Christ and the finished work of Christ on the cross. At the very least, they remind us that the Christian life is about living together as a community of believers. There is no escapism here, since, clearly, life has its struggles and problems (for example, Paul's imprisonment (4v3), the implicit challenge of speaking to non-believers in 4v5-6, and Paul's acknowledgment of the need for friends and colleagues in v4v11). Despite this, there is real confidence – confidence that praying to God makes a difference (4 v 2 and 4 v 12) and confidence that Christian ministry is, in essence, about serving the 'kingdom of God' (4 v 11). Most significant in the light of the whole letter is the subject of Epaphras' prayer in 4 v 12: 'that you may stand firm in all the will of God, mature and fully assured'. It was precisely this assurance that the Colossian false teachers undermined; and it is precisely this assurance that Paul sought to bolster and stabilise by writing to them.

OPTIONAL EXTRA
Consider doing some role-play in the group, as a way of helping people to be prepared for the difficult questions people commonly ask. Use this to sharpen one another up, especially in terms of aiding clarity in communicating gospel truths.

GUIDANCE ON QUESTIONS
2. Prayer: 'Being watchful' points to the need for dependence on God for both the opportunities and challenges of living in an unbelieving world. Being 'thankful' reminds us that, whatever our circumstances, there are always things to give praise to God for. Paul asks for prayer for gospel opportunities, but also that he prays for preaching clarity. This is a challenge and an encouragement. Paul needed it; so do we. But Paul also struggled to communicate the gospel - we should not think our difficulties in articulating the gospel mean we should not be doing it! We must also pray for open doors and clarity of gospel preaching for those who are specifically called to the work of evangelism.

Outreach: Look for God to open a door. Be prepared to proclaim the gospel clearly. Be prepared to suffer for it (Paul was 'in chains'). Live a godly life and be 'wise' towards outsiders (= think about how they think, so you can relate the gospel to them effectively). Be a good conversationalist.

Pastoral note: If people are overwhelmed by the challenge to share the gospel with others, remind them that the verses in this passage are all plural. In other words, the evangelistic effort is something that the church does as a whole, and so a variety of approaches and styles are valid. But clarity in the gospel is essential for us all. If people need help in this, challenge them to learn a simple gospel outline like *2 ways to live*.

3. This is the profound privilege of the Christian – Gentile or Jew – of knowing God in all His fullness in Christ. With false teachers on the prowl undermining this, no wonder Paul prays for clarity when he proclaims this. It suggests that the content of our message must be primarily about the person and work of our Lord Jesus Christ.

4. God is the one who opens doors (v 3). God is the one whose message is being preached – He kept it secret until the right time to open up the 'mystery of Christ' to the Gentile world (v 3), He gives the opportunities to proclaim it (v 5) and by implication is the one who provides answers to every question (v 6).

5. APPLY: Practical steps:

• It is helpful to keep prayer lists and prayer diaries, as well as to work systematically through the Bible so that we are challenged by its wide scope. If we are not praying for open doors or gospel opportunities, it is not likely that we will either notice or make the most of them when they come.

• As well as praying like this, we need to work hard at our clarity. Learning a gospel outline can help us to explain the gospel clearly. As does being prepared for different questions. It is perfectly reasonable to be caught out once – but it is irresponsible if we have not made an attempt to find answers and find that we are stumped by the same question twice.

• Again prayer is the key – so that we are depending on God for what we say. But it also means being proactive and looking for those opportunities to speak grace – which means both being gracious and speaking of the gospel grace of God.

6. Being part of the Christian family is a key theme: Tychicus is a dear brother (v 7) as is Onesimus (v 9). Yet most of the people are mentioned because of their faithfulness in gospel ministry, often at great personal cost: again Tychicus (v 7), Aristarchus (v 10), Mark and Jesus Justus (v 10-11), Epaphras (v 12).

7. Epaphras was persistent in prayer – Paul's word for 'wrestling' described the intense wrestling matches in the ancient world. There are connotations of Jacob wrestling with God (Genesis 32 v 22-32) – yet here Epaphras was doing it on the Colossians' behalf. It points to the urgency of their concern in the face of these false teachers (see 1 v 7; 1 v 29 – 2 v 1).

8. It reminds them that the message he preached cost him a great deal – but that in Paul's mind it was still worth it, such is the wonder of the gospel of the Christ, who is fully God dying to reconcile His universe. It is something therefore that the Colossians should also be prepared to suffer for.

EXPLORE MORE
Demas: The reference in 2 Tim 4 v 10 is a sad reminder that even active believers who are close to great teaching, enjoying Christian fellowship, and even in the thick of active Christian service, are still vulnerable to falling away. Use this cautionary tale to

remind your group that we need constantly to fight the holiness battles of chapter 3, or else the old self will reassert itself with potentially disastrous consequences.

9. APPLY: We need one another – teamwork and gospel partnership are vital. Prayer triplets are a great help for this – perhaps with a couple of others from the same office or neighbourhood. It is also good to have a close friend to whom we are accountable, a friend who has permission to ask us difficult questions about our personal walk and perseverance. Above all, we need to be part of a local Christian church both to serve and be served.

10. '**Stand firm':** Paul's main aim in writing this letter is to ensure that believers stand firm on the only solid rock there is: a full understanding of who Jesus Christ is and what He has done for and in us.
• **'In all the will of God':** a shallow understanding of the gospel will leave us open to false teaching, as it will create a dissatisfaction in our lives, that others will seek to exploit.
• **'Mature and fully assured':** by appreciating the greatness of Christ, and the fulness we have in Him.

11. These three scenarios will revise what people have learned in Colossians. Answers might include:
• The timid young Christian needs to understand exactly who he is following. Jesus is the creator and Lord of all creation, who has died and risen again for him. We are already secure and safe in heaven with Him.
• You will need to question the believer who has found 'something new'. If it is something that tries to add to, or subtract from the work of Christ, then they need to know that it is wrong. If it is a 'technique' they have discovered, they need to understand that it will have no power to change their hearts and lives. Only by sticking to the gospel and growing in an appreciation of it will they be truly changed and brought to maturity.
• In order to grow as a believer, we need to focus on Jesus and the gospel. Perhaps suggest that they work at the three marks of 3 v 15-17. Letting Christ's peace (ie: the gospel that has saved you) be the motivation for growing in godliness and relating to others. The word of Christ should be growing in you also, as you read and study the scriptures to know God and His will better. And a growing thankfulness to God for all things will be a mark of maturity.